BANK READY:

BREAKING THE LENDING CODE

2nd Edition

WILL M. CAMPBELL, JR., MA

An imprint of Campbell Publishing LLC.

Printed in the United States of America ISBN: 979-8-218-87350-9

This publication is designed to provide experienced based authoritative information regarding the subject matter covered. The publisher is not engaged in rendering psychological, financial, or legal service. It is sold with the understanding that if legal, financial, or any other professional counseling assistance is needed in any area, it should be sought.

For information about speaking engagements or interviews contact us via email at BREAKINGTHELENDINGCODE@GMAIL.COM

ACKNOWLEDGEMENTS

I would like to express my deepest gratitude to the Almighty, my Lord and Savior, for providing me with the strength, wisdom, and inspiration throughout this journey. Your divine guidance has been my source of comfort and perseverance.

To my beloved wife, Myra (Mary) Campbell, your unwavering support, encouragement, and understanding have been the pillars that held me up during the challenging times. Your love is my greatest blessing, and I am forever grateful for your presence in my life.

A heartfelt thank you goes to my mentor, Elder Irvine Armstrong, whose wisdom and guidance have shaped my perspective and fueled my aspirations. Your teachings have been invaluable, and I am privileged to have had you as a guiding force.

To my dear children, Will, David, and Maya Campbell, your love and understanding during moments of absence have meant the world to me. Your resilience and joy have been a constant reminder of what truly matters in life. I am proud to be your Dad.

Special thanks to my attorney and friend, Eugene Radcliff, for your legal expertise, steadfast support, and unwavering friendship. Your counsel has been instrumental in navigating the complexities of this endeavor, and I am grateful for the bond we share.

This book is a culmination of the support and encouragement I have received from these remarkable individuals. I am blessed to have such a wonderful circle of family, friends, and mentors who have contributed to the realization of this project. Thank you all for being an integral part of my journey.

CONTENTS

INTRODUCTION

OUR LOAN HAS BEEN APPROVED," is a phrase you want to hear as an entrepreneur attempting to start or grow your business. Unfortunately, many will not hear these words due to fear and lack of confidence in presenting themselves and their business to a lender. If you are exhibiting this fear or you have personally faced the crushing disappointment of hearing the words, "YOUR LOAN IS DENIED," this book is for you. As both a lender and a passionate advocate for small businesses, I possess firsthand knowledge on how to break the lending code. With my expertise, I am fully equipped to assist you in securing the necessary funds to initiate or expand your business ventures successfully.

While working within some of the largest financial institutions and counseling small businesses for over 30 years, I have learned the common hurdles faced by most small businesses in obtaining capital. These obstacles include insufficient preparation when applying for loans, subpar business and personal credit, inadequate cash flow, absence of collateral, limited business management expertise, improper tax filing, and inaccurate financial record keeping.

For these and many other reasons, I decided to write this book. My unwavering passion lies in serving the small business community, as I firmly believe it is my purpose and destined path. This book is meant for the everyday small business owner - the AC company owner, the plumbing companies, painters, contractors, physicians, daycare facility owners, healthcare providers, auto mechanics, etc.

I will cover the three key areas that will equip you to break the code and obtain the resources needed to grow. These key areas include thorough guidance on loan preparation, navigating the loan processing stage, and fulfilling post-loan requirements.

In this book, you will learn to understand the basic lending process. It will equip you to understand the lender's mind, eye, and heartbeat. Most importantly, you will understand how to break the lending code to obtain access to capital to fund your business.

CHAPTER 1

ISSUES BUSINESSES FACE

Over the last 30 years, as a Senior Vice President for several banks, financial services agencies, and entrepreneurial consulting organizations (such as Wells Fargo, Bank One, Liberty Bank, Small Business Development Center (SBDC), Capital One Bank, Essential Federal Credit Union, and b1Bank), I saw thousands of small businesses struggle to gain access to capital for growth. According to the U.S Small Business Administration (2022), 99.9% of all businesses in the United States qualify as small businesses, collectively employing 46.4% of the nation's private workforce. Unfortunately, they were one of the hardest hit sectors of the economy during the COVID-19 Pandemic, leaving many small businesses closed. Billions of dollars from the CARES ACT have been allocated to help small businesses.

Many small businesses still need help to stay afloat, keep their doors open and gain access to capital. There is a clear connection between a small business owner's ability to expand and the need for access to capital. Based on my experience as a seasoned lender, gaining access to capital has been a significant problem for small businesses in the United

States. Many factors affect a business owner's lack of access to capital. These factors can range from a low credit score, the inability to provide debt service coverage, and the lack of cash flow and collateral to a lack of liquidity. My goal is to help small business owners break the lending code and help bring their dreams to reality.

Listed below are a few memorable moments in helping entrepreneurs bring their dreams to reality:

1. a nurse practitioner that sought to expand her special needs pediatric clinic was able to obtain a $1,100,000 loan to construct a new facility.
2. a local restaurant expanded and opened a 2nd location with a loan totaling over $250,000.
3. a local small painting company obtained a $50,000 working capital line of credit.

So, let's dive further into understanding the issues businesses face. Listed here are eight crucial issues that a small business owner should have knowledge of:

1. Gaining access to capital - Three primary barriers include the disappearance of small community banks and larger banks unwilling to make loans under $150,000, the lack of collateral, and venture capital investors only focusing on high-growth potential companies.
2. Obtaining affordable health care - Managing healthcare for employees is challenging. The increased cost makes it difficult to manage. While Obamacare endows workers' health benefits, business owners often face the financial blow.
3. Paying taxes - taxes are complicated. Many business owners need help understanding how their tax liability is determined. Many small business owners need to learn the corporate tax rate, what tax cuts they are eligible for, and what past-due income tax means. In addition

to income taxes, business owners must pay payroll, unemployment, and other taxes. To make things even more complicated, tax laws can change from year to year. This can be very overwhelming to a small business owner.

4. Securing affordable business insurance - Unfortunately, many small businesses are not covered. From my years of experience, I can attest that many small business owners have never purchased business insurance. By purchasing the correct insurance, you can protect your company from damages and legal claims. Many small business owners give up on insurance because of how confusing and expensive the process can be.

5. Hiring experienced personnel - One of the most significant challenges faced by businesses is the issue of labor quality. Finding skilled individuals who are the right fit for the job can be a daunting task. This poses a critical risk, especially considering that the majority of challenges can only be overcome with an exceptional team that collaborates to effectively achieve the business's goal. When you have high employee turnover, you spend more money hiring new talent, affecting the company's profit margin.

6. Maximizing growth opportunities - In time, a business may boom beyond growth expectations. Small business owners with no plan for the increase in customers and the related need for an increase in product/service production are liable to fall by the wayside. As demand for business increases, without a proper system in place, you're most likely to come up short and fall short of meeting client demand. Therefore, scaling up your business is crucial.

7. Managing cash flow - Effective cash flow management can be very challenging for small business owners and cause problems. One tip

is to keep track of your money, where it's coming from, and where it's heading. Many small business owners must learn how to manage their daily cash flow.

8. Economic conditions - Not even wall street brokers genuinely know how the economy will pan out. The uncertainty of economic conditions cannot be understated and deserves the utmost respect. For example, the global COVID-19 Pandemic greatly impacted the small business community. During the pandemic, many small businesses either swiftly pivoted to survive or struggled to stay afloat.

As a small business owner, you must realize that all these areas can affect the profitability of your business. Therefore, it is essential to maintain accurate financials to ensure that when you apply for a business loan, you have adequate cash flow to finance future growth. You must refrain from allowing your accountant to drive profitability by trying to pay fewer taxes.

Still confused? Let's talk more about the most significant challenges for your business — having access to capital, cash flow, and understanding credit. Even if access becomes available, the issue then flows to managing cash flow and maintaining credit.

Small businesses are the major entrepreneurship drivers, accounting for all sales growth. It makes up most of all businesses in the local economy. According to the Small Business Administration (SBA) (2022), small business makes up about 99.9% of revenue in the United States. The criteria to identify as a small business is one with 500 or fewer employees; Most small businesses have less than 10 employees. The success of our economy is linked to the success of the small business community. For example, John Doe L.L.C. is a local janitorial service provider and has been in business for 20 years, with 10 employees, and generated approximately $500,000 in revenue annually. This is an example of the size and revenue standard of most small businesses that operate in the United States.

A small business could only be successful or last past a year with access to capital. Capital refers to the adequacy of funds the company employs to operate efficiently in generating cash flow. Most business owners run businesses using credit cards, personal finances, loans from friends and family, and current earnings. How do you get from knowing that you need working capital to having a business bank account? You have lots of questions, and the process can be daunting for many reasons. From a lender's perspective, some key elements are necessary before stepping into an office to request a loan. Access to capital is the lifeline to helping a small business have longevity. Access to capital is a major challenge for all small businesses nationwide. Most small businesses are challenged with gaining capital due to the need for more cash flow (cash).

Even further, the lack of access to capital among minority entrepreneurs has been well documented by several sources. Again, the reason for this is the lack of knowledge on how the banking system works, not understanding how to read financial statements, having a personal credit score of less than 640, lack of assets, no fundamental knowledge on how to manage a business from a financial perspective, not having an accountant (bookkeeper) on staff, and not filing taxes properly (filing taxes properly means showing the lender your company has enough debt service creditability).

As the research identifies, overcoming barriers to accessing capital begins with education. Small business owners perish for lack of knowledge.

> **A big barrier to overcome, according to a U. S. Bank (2020), is cash flow. The company states that a whopping 82% of businesses fail because of cash flow problems.**

Remember, cash flow does not mean the amount of money coming in and out. You must also take timing into account. For example, if you operate a business based on an invoicing system and your invoices have yet to be collected, and your loan payments are due; if you don't have a cash flow reserve, you might end up with a cash flow problem. (Once you have invoiced a company, this turns into an accounts receivable, which can vary in days due. The company will need enough liquidity (cash) to sustain itself during the invoice/receivable period.

Let me paint a bigger picture. Let's say a subcontractor such as ABC Electrical Company is a company that is working for XYZ General Contracting Firm. General Firm pays invoices every 45 days. ABC Electrical has ten employees who get paid weekly, so the company needs adequate cash to cover payroll until XYZ General pays its invoice. Therefore, if ABC Electrical does not have a line of credit to sustain them for 45 days until they receive payment from XYZ General Firm, they will be in a cash flow crunch. This will disrupt operations and put the company in a bind. ABC Electric must always maintain adequate liquidity (cash) to avoid cash flow problems.

ABC Electrical can run into cash flow problems if more capital is needed to sustain themselves between jobs. The issue is not the payments or making a profit; the issue is managing and having enough cash flow (cash). Most companies are paid on a net of a 30, 45, or 60-day basis. The subcontractor would need to sustain themselves for that period with cash reserves or a working capital line of credit.

There are three primary financial statements bankers use to check the financial health of your business. They are (1) balance sheet, (2) profit and loss/income statement, and (3) cash flow statement. The balance sheet shows what a company owns and owes at a fixed point in time. It gives a snapshot of how healthy your company is. It also shows total shareholders' equity. An income statement lists all sales generated and expenses during a specific period. It also shows the net profit or the difference between sales and expenses. Income statements are generally managed monthly. The cash flow statement reconciles the balance sheet and the income statement. It reports accounts for the movement of cash in and out of the business. The cash flow statement shows a company's cash transactions (Inflow & Outflow) within a specific period.

Let's look at the first three financial statements in more detail.

Balance Sheet

A balance sheet provides detailed information about the company's assets, liabilities, and shareholder's equity.

Assets are things that a company owns that have value. This typically means they can either be sold or used by the company to make products or provide services that can be sold. Assets include physical property, such as plants, trucks, equipment, and inventory. It also includes things that can't be touched but exist and have value, such as trademarks and patents. Cash itself is an asset. So are the investments a company makes.

Liabilities are amounts of money that a company owes to others. This can include all kinds of obligations, like money borrowed from a bank to launch a new product, rent for the use of a building, money owed to suppliers for materials, payroll a company owes its employees, environmental clean- up cost, or taxes owed to the government. Liabilities also include obligations to provide future goods or services to customers.

Shareholder's equity is sometimes called capital or net worth. The money that would be left if a company sold its assets and paid off all its liabilities. This leftover money belongs to shareholders or the company's owners.

The following formula summarizes what a balance sheet shows:

$$Assets = Liabilities + Shareholder's\ Equity$$

A company's assets must equal or balance the sum of its liabilities and shareholders' equity.

A company's balance sheet is set up like the basic accounting equation shown above. On the left side of the balance sheet, companies list their assets. On the right side, they list their liabilities and shareholders' equity.

Assets are generally listed based on how quickly they will be converted into cash. Current assets are things a company expects to convert to cash within one year. A good example is inventory. Noncurrent assets are things a company does not anticipate will convert to cash within one year or would take longer than one year to sell. Noncurrent assets include fixed assets. Fixed assets are those used to operate the business but not available for sale, such as trucks, office furniture, and other property.

Liabilities are generally listed based on their due dates. Liabilities are said to be either current or long-term. Current liabilities are obligations a company expects to pay off within the year. Long-term liabilities are obligations due more than one year away.

Shareholders' equity is the amount owners invested in the company's stock plus or minus the company's earnings or losses since inception. Sometimes companies distribute profits, instead of retaining them. These distributions are called dividends.

A balance sheet shows a snapshot of a company's assets, liabilities, and shareholders' equity at the end of the reporting period. It does not show the flows into and out of the accounts during the period.

	Pre Start-up Position	Month 1	Month 2	Month 3	Month 4	Month 5	Month 6	Month 7	Month 8	Month 9	Month 10	Month 11	Month 12	Total
ASSETS														
Current Assets:														
Cash														
Investments (Marketable Securities)														
Accounts Receivable														
Inventory														
Prepaid Expenses														
Other (specify each)														
Total Current Assets														
Fixed Assets:														
Land														
Buildings														
Leasehold Improvements														
Furniture/Fixtures														
Machinery & Equipment														
Vehicles (Autos & Trucks)														
Less Accumulated Depreciation & Amort.														
Total Net Fixed Assets														
Other (specify each)														
Total Assets														
LIABILITIES														
Current Liabilities:														
Notes Payable--Bank														
Current Portion of Long-Term Debt														
Accounts Payable--Trade														
Accruals (payroll)														
Income Taxes Payable														
Other (specify each)														
Total Current Liabilities														
Long-Term Liabilities:														
Notes Payable														
Other (specify each)														
Total Long-Term Liabilities														
Total Liabilities														
NET WORTH														
Owner Equity														
Capital Stock														
Additional Paid-In Capital														
Retained Earnings														
Total Net Worth														
Total Liabilities and Net Worth														

Profit and Loss Statement

The profit and loss statement (P&L), or income statement, is a financial report that summarizes a company's revenue, expenses, and profits/losses over a given period. The P&L statement shows a company's ability to generate sales, manage expenses, and create profit. A P&L statement is prepared based on accounting principles that include revenue recognition, matching, and accruals, which makes it different from the cash flow statement.

Revenues - Expenses = Profit or Loss

A company's profit and loss statement is recorded over a specific period, typically a month, quarter, or fiscal year.

The main categories that can be found on the P&L include:

- Revenue
- Cost of Goods Sold
- Selling, General & Administrative Expenses
- Marketing and Advertising
- Technology/Research & Development
- Interest Expense
- Taxes
- Net Income

Profit and Loss/Income Statements also report earnings per share (EPS). This calculation tells you how much money shareholders would receive if the company distributed all the net revenues for the period. Companies rarely distribute all their earnings. Usually, they reinvest in the business.

To understand how income statements are set up, think of them as a set of stairs. You start at the top with total sales made during the accounting period. Then you go down, one step at a time. At each stage, you deduct certain costs or other operating expenses associated with earning revenue. After deducting all expenses, when you reach the bottom of the stairs, you learn how much the company made or lost during the accounting period. People often call this "the bottom line."

At the top of the Profit and Loss/Income statement is the total amount of money brought in from sales of products or services. This top line is often referred to as gross revenues or sales. It's called "gross" because expenses have not been deducted from it yet, so the number is "gross" or unrefined.

The following line is money the company doesn't expect to collect on certain sales. This could be due, for example, to sale discounts or merchandise returns.

You arrive at the company's revenues when subtracting the returns and allowances from the gross revenues. This is called "net".

Several lines request various kinds of operating expenses when moving down the stairs from the net revenue line. Although these lines can be reported in various order, the next line after net revenues typically shows sales costs. This number tells you how much the company spent to produce the goods it sold during the accounting period.

The following line subtracts the cost of sales from the net revenues to arrive at a subtotal called "gross profit" or "gross margin." It is considered "gross" because certain expenses have not been deducted.

The next section deals with operating expenses. These are expenses that go toward supporting a company's operations for a given period - for example, the salaries of administrative personnel and the cost of researching new products. Marketing expenses are another example. Operating expenses cannot be linked directly to the production of the products or services being sold.

Depreciation is also deducted from gross profit. Depreciation accounts for the wear and tear on some assets, such as machinery, tools, and furniture, used over the long term. Companies spread the cost of these assets over the periods in which they are used. The process of spreading these costs is called depreciation or amortization. The "charge" for using these assets during the period is a fraction of the original costs of assets.

After all operating expenses are deducted from gross profit, you arrive at operating profit before interest and income tax expenses. This is often called "income from operations."

Next, companies must account for interest income and interest expenses. Interest income is the money companies make from keeping their cash in interest-bearing savings accounts, money market funds, and other similar savings tools. On the other hand, interest expense is the money companies pay in interest for the money they borrow. Some income statements show interest income and interest expenses separately. Some income statements combine these two numbers. The interest income and expenditures are then added and subtracted from the operating profits to arrive at operating profit before income tax.

Finally, income tax is deducted, and you arrive at the bottom line: net profit or net losses. Net profit is also called net income or net earnings. This tells you how much the company earned or lost during the accounting period. Did the company make a profit, or did it lose money?

Example of an Income Statement

	Month 1	Month 2	Month 3	Month 4	Month 5	Month 6	Month 7	Month 8	Month 9	Month 10	Month 11	Month 12	Total	%
GROSS REVENUE (Sales or Fees):														
TOTAL GROSS REVENUE														
Less Returns, Allowances, & Discounts														
NET SALES REVENUE														
Less COST OF GOODS SOLD:														
GROSS PROFIT														
OPERATING EXPENSES:														
Salaries & Wages														
Commissions														
Payroll Taxes & Benefits														
Security														
Promotion (advertising, etc.)														
Vehicle & Delivery														
Dues & Subscriptions														
Accounting & Legal Fees														
Office Supplies														
Operating Supplies														
Maintenance & Repairs														
Travel & Entertainment														
Rent														
Telephone														
Utilities														
Insurance														
Taxes (property, etc.)														
Depreciation & Amortization														
Selling (check/credit card fee, etc.)														
Bad Debts														
Other (specify each)														
Miscellaneous														
TOTAL OPERATING EXPENSES														
Total Operating Income (EBIT)														
+ Other Revenue (interest income, etc.)														
- Other Expenses (interest, etc.)														
NET PROFIT (LOSS) before taxes														
- Taxes														

Cash Flow Statement

Cash flow statements report a company's inflows and outflows of cash. This is important because a company must have enough cash on hand to pay its expenses and purchase assets. While an income statement can tell you whether a company made a profit, a cash flow statement can tell you whether the company generated cash.

A cash flow statement shows changes over time rather than absolute dollar amounts at a point in time. It uses and reorders the information from a company's balance sheet and income statement.

The bottom line of the cash flow statement shows the net increases and decreases in cash for the period. Generally, cash flow statements are divided into three main parts. Each part reviews the cash flow from one of three types of activities:

(1) operating activities; (2) investing activities ; and (3) financing activities.

Operating Activities

The first part of a cash flow statement analyzes a company's cash flow from net income or losses. For most companies, this section of the cash flow statement reconciles the net income (as shown on the income statement) to the actual cash the company received from or used in its operating activities. To do this, it modifies the net income for non-cash items (such as adding back depreciation expenses) and adjusts for any cash used or provided by other operating assets and liabilities.

Investing Activities

The second part of the cash flow statement shows the cash flow from all investing activities, generally including purchases or sales of long-term assets, such as property, equipment, and investment securities. Suppose a company buys a piece of machinery. The cash flow statement should reflect this activity as a cash outflow from investing activities because it used cash. If the company decided to sell off some investments from an investment portfolio, the proceeds from the sales would show up as cash flow from investing activities because it provided cash.

Financing Activities

The third part of a cash flow statement shows the cash flow from all financing activities. Typical sources of cash flows include cash raised by selling stocks and bonds or borrowing from banks. Likewise, paying back a bank loan would show up as a use of cash flow.

Cash Flow = The difference between the available cash at the accounting period's beginning and end. Cash comes in from sales, loan proceeds, investments, and the sale of assets and goes out to pay for operating and direct expenses, principal debt service, and purchases.

Incoming and outgoing cash represents the operating activities of the business. Cash is very important because it allows you to pay for things needed to run your business, such as mortgage or lease payments, payroll, materials, and other operational expenses. There are two types of cash flow, positive cash flow, and negative cash flow. Positive cash flow is more money coming in versus going out. Negative cash flow is more money going out than coming in. The cash flow statement shows how a company has performed when cash enters the business (cash inflows) and when cash goes out (cash outflows). It provides a cleaner picture of a company's ability to pay lenders and finance growth.

Sample Cash Flow Statement

	Pre Start-up Position	Month 1	Month 2	Month 3	Month 4	Month 5	Month 6	Month 7	Month 8	Month 9	Month 10	Month 11	Month 12	Total
CASH ON HAND (Beginning of month)														
CASH RECEIPTS:														
Cash Sales														
Collections from Credit Accounts														
Loan or Other Cash Injection														
TOTAL CASH RECEIPTS														
TOTAL CASH AVAILABLE														
CASH DISBURSEMENTS:														
Purchases (inventory)														
Salaries & Wages														
Commissions														
Payroll Taxes & Benefits														
Security														
Promotion (advertising, etc.)														
Vehicle & Delivery														
Dues & Subscriptions														
Accounting & Legal Fees														
Office Supplies														
Operating Supplies														
Maintenance & Repairs														
Travel & Entertainment														
Rent														
Telephone														
Utilities														
Insurance														
Taxes (property tax, etc.)														
Selling (check/credit card fee, etc.)														
Other Expenses (specify each)														
Miscellaneous														
SUBTOTAL (cash out for operating costs)														
Debt Service (loan payment)														
Capital Purchases (specify each)														
Other Start-up Costs														
Reserve and/or Escrow (specify each)														
Owner's Withdrawal														
TOTAL CASH DISBURSEMENTS														
CASH POSITION (End of month)														

The cash flow statement stands as the most indispensable tool for small businesses due to the following reasons:

1. Cash flow is the lifeline for a small business. If cash flow is a problem for a business, the owner cannot secure a loan against its assets. The business owner will miss growth opportunities.

2. Lenders look at operating cash flow to determine if a business can secure a loan.

3. Positive cash flow will allow a business to be proactive in growth opportunities. It allows the lender to grant expansion loans, lines of credit, etc.

4. Having cash in the bank is the greatest asset of a small business

owner. It opens a world of opportunity for the small business owner.

5. Good cash flow management means a very healthy business future.

Definitions to Know

1. Earnings Before Interest, Taxes, Depreciation, and Amortization (EBITDA) is a measure of the business cash flow that looks at earnings/net income + non-cash changes.
2. Debt Service (DS) is the annual principal and interest.
3. Debt Service Coverage (DSC) measures a business's cash flow available to service debt.
4. Debt Service Coverage Ratio (DSCR) measures a business's capacity to pay its debt(s) on time. It answers whether there is enough cash flow to pay all loan payments.
5. Loan to Value (LTV) ratio is expressed as a percentage of the principal amount of the subject loan to the fair market value of the asset securing the loan.

Understanding Credit

There is a difference between personal credit and business credit. Once you understand how lenders operate, you can then work on your credit as a tool to build funds. A business owner must have good credit (a score of at least 640, for reference).

If you are like most small business owners, your personal and business credit scores are something you really don't think about. You need a good personal credit score to qualify for a business loan, line of credit, or credit card. Remember, a bad credit score can affect your personal and business life. However, a bad credit score is not permanent. By following a few simple rules, you can clean up your credit history and rebuild your good name. Your credit score is based on five key factors:

1. Payment history - Lenders want to know if you will repay the money

you borrow. Also, whether you pay on time or as agreed. If you miss payments, your score goes down. Your payment history makes up 35% of your total credit score.

2. Amount of debt - Using up every bit of your available credit is a sign that you are stretched too thin and have cash flow issues. The debt you owe on credit cards and loans makes up 30% of your credit score.

3. Length of credit history - Your credit history makes up 15% of your credit score. It looks very good in the eyes of a lender when a borrower has been using credit and paying it back for an extended amount of time.

4. Credit mix - A borrower with different types of loans, such as a mortgage, auto loan, and credit cards, looks better than just having one or two credit cards. The credit mix makes up 10% of your credit score.

5. Credit inquiries account for about 10% of your credit score. Every time a borrower wants to take out a loan, it affects their credit score. If you attempt to take out a new loan, it hurts your credit score.

Fair, Isaac and Company (FICO) was the entity that developed the system for scoring credit in 1958 (Herron, 2013). The system wasn't widely accepted as the industry standard in lending until 1989. Credit scores are calculated by adding all factors (payment history, amount of debt, credit history length, credit mix, and credit inquiries). Scores range from 300-850.

Today, several credit score companies (all employing the FICO system) are used by lenders nationwide. The most trusted of these are Equifax, TransUnion, and Experian. Their websites are listed below:

www.equifax.com

www.transunion.com

www.experian.com

In preparing for a loan, you must understand the 5 Cs of credit. Getting a loan approved is based on many factors, including the risk that the lender takes on. Those factors are called the five Cs of credit — character, capacity, capital, conditions, and collateral.

- Character - determined by how well you pay your bills, especially during hard times.
- Capacity - the ability to pay your debt obligations.
- Capital - having enough funds in your business to operate daily. Another name for capital is called liquidity.
- Conditions - the factors of the economy and environment that may affect your business.
- Collateral -an asset that can be pledged to secure a loan.

Lenders will review your credit history to determine your overall creditworthiness. Your ability to secure a loan approval will be hindered if a lender or creditor sees several late payments or other negative factors such as collection accounts, charge-offs, or judgments. There are more severe types of derogatory credit, such as bankruptcies and foreclosures. They may limit your loan options for an extended period.

Understanding the Credit Scoring System

Small business owners need to know how credit works. Credit scoring is a mathematical equation that evaluates many types of information by comparing that data to patterns of hundreds of thousands of past periods. The score identifies risk. You must have at least one credit account that has been open for at least six months before a FICO score can be generated.

Each major credit agency, such as Equifax, TransUnion, and Experian, will provide a FICO score to a lender. The higher the score, the lower the risk. The FICO score only looks at information on your credit report. It can report positively or negatively on you as a person. Keep a good name with your credit score. Proverbs 22:1 says, "A good name is more desirable than great riches; to be esteemed is better than silver or gold."

FICO Score Breakdown

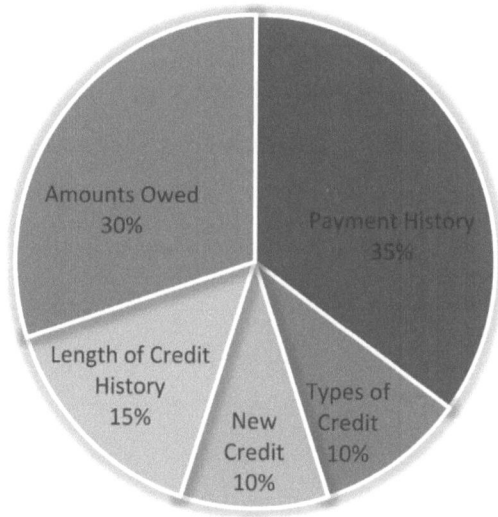

Amounts Owed
30%

Payment History
35%

Length of Credit History
15%

New Credit
10%

Types of Credit
10%

Credit Score Shelf Life

Positive credit is indefinite. Late payments, collections, Chapter 11 & 13 bankruptcies, foreclosures, unpaid taxes, judgments, student loans, and debt remain in your credit file for seven years. Inquiries stay recorded for two years and Chapter 7 bankruptcy remains for ten years. The older the negative item, the less impact it has on your credit score.

How to Build Credit

Here are a few ways that you can increase your credit score. Be patient, review your report annually, dispute incorrect items, monitor your credit mix (based on the chart above), pay your bills on time, and stay current on payments. Be cautious of paying off/closing a collections account on which you've previously missed a payment. These actions alone will not remove an unfavorable statement from your credit report (if you are having trouble making payments on time, please consult your lender immediately).

Always keep your credit card balances under 30% of your credit limit. Pay off debt rather than move it around (DO NOT transfer/consolidate debt to another lender). Do not close unused credit cards or open a new credit card if you don't need it. Remember, a mixture of credit is healthy.

Other ways to build business credit include paying your suppliers on time, purchasing items in your business name, and ensuring that your business credit is reported to Duns & Bradstreet (D&B). Also, make sure Equifax is reporting your business credit.

How to Obtain a Copy of Your Credit Report

As a lender with over 30 years of experience, I recommend obtaining a free copy of your credit report from www.creditreport.com. This will help you monitor your credit health and mitigate any risk of credit fraud. Download a request form at www.annualcreditreport.com or call 877-322-8228. Once downloaded and completed, the annual credit report request form should be mailed to:

Annual Credit Report Request Services

P.O. Box 105281, Atlanta, Georgia 30348-5281

CHAPTER 2

THINK LIKE A LENDER: WHERE TO BORROW

Access to working capital is needed to ensure that a business owner has enough cash flow to operate. The following are reasons why a business owner needs to borrow money:

- To have working capital so the business has enough cash flow to operate daily. It should be used for payroll, purchasing, supplies, etc.
- To have business acquisition funds to purchase another business operation (ex., Business A will get a loan to buy Business B).
- To purchase business equipment or vehicles needed to run a business.
- To purchase rental or investment property to gain additional income.
- To make leasehold improvements on a leased space used to run and operate a business (ex., the tenant obtains a loan to improve the property they are renting, such as changing flooring, raising ceilings, and adding additional office space. The tenant is also responsible for taking their signage and other business-related movables with them when they leave).

- To obtain a business credit card used to purchase business items. The interest should be paid on the bill every month.
- For business expansion, when a business reaches the point for growth.

The top funding sources for small business owners include banks, credit unions, venture capitalists, angel investors, commercial brokers, micro-lenders, and personal investors.

Bank or Credit Union

The difference between a bank and a credit union is banks are for-profit, meaning they are privately owned or publicly traded, while credit unions are non-profit institutions. Credit unions have members, and banks have customers. Generally, credit union members have lower rates on loans and fees. Most credit unions do not make commercial loans. Banks also have a wider variety of products and services for small business owners versus credit unions. Banks offer lines of credit, commercial real estate, and equipment loans.

Additional Funding Sources

- Commercial Brokers
- Venture Capitalists
- Angel Investors
- Microlenders
- Factoring Companies

Unlocking the Mind of the Lender

Lenders analyze the following:

- Risks
- Cash Flow
- Credit History

- Liquidity
- Experience in working within a particular industry.
- Economy
- Loan concentration mix
- Loan to value ratios

Think Like a Lender (the Mind of a Lender) Lenders usually reviews the following:

- RMA (Risk Management Association) data to obtain benchmark and industry trend data.
- DUNS report to obtain business credit history.
- Complete Uniform Commercial Code (UCC) search to check for possible liens on the businesses.
- Reference checks with suppliers and other creditors
- Extensive background and reference checks regarding a potential borrower's character from Social Media, Better Business Bureau, Clerk of Courts, Business Websites, etc.

Perspective of a Lender (the Eye of a Lender) Things lenders usually look at:

- Cash Flow
- Liquidity
- Debt to Service Coverage Ratios
- Business and Personal Credit
- Collateral
- Industry Management Experience of the Borrower
- Type of Industry (high or low risk)
- Longevity in the Business Market
- Net Worth (both business and personal)
- Relationship with the Lender

- Number of Deposits
- Loan Payment History
- Good Character
- Solid Business Plan or Growth Plan

Work Like a Lender (Hand of the Lender)

Things the lender usually does:

- Walks the borrower through the lending process.
- Helps prepare the loan package.
- Pulls business and personal credit reports.
- Analyzes the borrower's credit report.
- Helps structure the loan.
- Determines the amount of money needed.
- Determines the type of loan needed.
- Determines what collateral will be used.
- Determines the amount of cash flow to debt service of the loan request.
- Determines how much borrower qualifies for based on cash flow.
- Acts as a personal advisor that helps manage the success of the business.
- Performs annual reviews to ensure continued success.

Now that we have explored the issues that small businesses encounter, let's delve further into why a small business should borrow money. We'll discuss the best funding sources, character building and the significance of fostering strong relationships with lenders.

CHAPTER 3

PREPARING FOR A LOAN

It is important that you place yourself in the best possible position to have a good name with lenders. A big nugget to remember is that your name aligns with having good credit; when you show a lender your credit, you prove that you are a viable business owner.

Remember these words from Proverbs 22:1 – "a good name is to be chosen rather than great riches. Loving favor rather than silver and gold." Your credit score gives a snapshot of the status of your name. Do you care how credit bureaus, bank lenders, suppliers, and investors view your name? A good name really speaks to your integrity. It is about your reputation and the character on the inside of you. It demonstrates your morals and business ethics from a personal standpoint. Essentially, character and credit are one and the same, it defines who you are.

1. A good name (credit) provides stability. It says a lender can trust you.
2. A good name (credit) is eternal. It follows you all the days of your life.
3. A good name (credit) brings loving favor. Paying bills as agreed.

Lenders choose you for having financial integrity.

Most lenders' philosophies are based on a trend analysis of a borrower's ability to repay the debt obligation. A trend develops over time ranging from three months to over three years. The lender's job is to evaluate the business owner's financial direction and ability to repay debt obligations.

How to Prepare for a Loan

1. Build a solid relationship with a lender. Choose a personable and intelligent lender with a servant's heart and passion for business lending. Some lenders are specialty lenders and have a vested industry-specific interest. How do you find the right lender?

    a. Referrals

    b. Networking

2. Choose a lender with a community feel and a city flavor. If you generate revenue at $500,000 or less per year, get a lender who will spend time with you to understand business's mission and vision. Local lenders demonstrate a distinct dedication to supporting the local and state economy, fostering job creation, and upholding their commitment to the local marketplace.

3. Choose a lender who goes beyond their role as a lender and functions as a business consultant. Find one who is invested in your growth while remaining bankable and profitable. Finding such a lender is akin to having a valuable team member who supports you from within, rather than an external entity solely providing funds.

4. Most lenders today do not have an entrepreneurial mindset. They only see from a lender's perspective. Your loan will be denied if the credit request does not fit into the lender's credit policy. Also, try to find a lender who can meet your needs during the dating period. Find

out about the lender's appetite. What type of loans do they approve and hold in their portfolio? Also, what specific kind of businesses do they lend to? Below are some examples of high-risk businesses that most lenders prefer not to lend to:

a. Startups

b. Contractors

c. Trucking Companies

d. Religious Institutions

e. Gaming Companies

f. Residential and Commercial Contracting

g. Car Dealerships

h. Money Services

How you look on paper is very important to loan approvers. Lenders look at your loan documents to determine their level of risk, so I want to reiterate the importance of you establishing your business and business credit legitimately.

Take what is needed for a lender to process a loan, and you will understand why:

1. The borrower must fill out a complete loan application.

2. The borrower must give the history of the business.

3. Management's resume should outline industry experience.

4. Business debt, schedule

5. Interim financial statements

6. All borrowers must submit a personal financial statement (PFS). The PFS should list the detailed assets, liabilities, real estate, marketable and nonmarketable securities, etc.

7. The lender will need a minimum of two years of both business and personal tax returns. Three years are preferred. If more than one

borrower is listed on the loan application, each person should submit their personal tax returns.

BENEFITS OF FILING ACCURATE TAX RETURNS

- It gives the lender a true and accurate picture of the cash flow to calculate debt. It also provides an accurate accounting of how the business is performing.
- It helps to secure the capital needed to operate your business.
- It demonstrates the actual historical financial position of the business.
- It keeps you out of trouble with the IRS.
- It gives you an accurate picture of the business profitability if you desire to sell.

WHY IS IT IMPORTANT TO THE LENDER?

It provides details to the lender to perform annual reviews.

DOES A GUARANTOR HAVE TO HAVE OWNERSHIP IN THE BUSINESS?

Yes

WHEN SHOULD AN ENTREPRENEUR BORROW MONEY?

Entrepreneurs should borrow money when they don't need it or during business expansions and renovations.

NOTES:

_____

_____

_____

_____

_____

_____

_____

_____

_____

_____

_____

_____

_____

_____

_____

_____

_____

_____

_____

CHAPTER 4

PROCESSING OF YOUR LOAN

If you have been running your business for a while, are interested in purchasing a building, buying equipment, or require working capital, you must pay close attention to the following information.

From my years of experience working with clients, I know the commercial loan process can be very intimidating. By walking through the steps below, you will learn how to make the commercial loan process seamless.

How the Commercial Loan Process Works

When you submit your business loan application, it may seem like it disappears into a black hole. Understanding how the commercial loan system works can help reduce your anxiety or stress while you wait for approval.

Some lenders like to prequalify potential borrowers to determine how much they can afford. This will allow you and your lender an opportunity to see which loan program would be most appropriate for your needs. The lender will gather basic information, such as your income and debts.

You must complete and submit a loan application to initiate the loan process. Once your application is received, a loan officer or processor will review your credit reports, collateral amount, and income. Your loan officer will determine if additional documentation, such as personal financial statements, is required. If you are purchasing real estate, you may also need to submit preliminary environmental reports, area maps, title reports, property appraisals, and lease summaries. If you are going through a broker, they will package your loan request and submit it to several lenders for review and approval.

After submitting your commercial loan package to the decision-makers, a loan committee, underwriter, or processor will present a letter of intent or term sheet. This formal document ensures that all parties (lender and business owner) are on the same page.

The letter of intent may include the name of the involved parties, the amount of financing, the type of security (collateral), and other key terms. Decisions are usually made in 1 to 15 business days. During the underwriting process, you may need to furnish additional documentation. If you are using a broker, he or she should be helping you negotiate the best terms and conditions from various lenders. The next step is choosing the most attractive offer and signing and returning the final letter of intent to the lender, along with a checking account number, if required, for a deposit and to pay for third- party reports, such as appraisals, surveys, title reports, etc.

After all third-party reports are completed, and underwriting conditions are satisfied, the loan package is resubmitted for final approval. At this point, the lender will issue a final full loan commitment. If your loan is approved, your closing agent (an attorney, a title company, or an escrow company representative) will receive closing documents. Your closing agent will record the mortgage, obtain title insurance, coordinate the exchange of funds, and arrange for you to sign the loan documents. Closing can take place within days of approval of underwriting. At closing, the lender funds the loan with a cashier's check or electronic wire transfer.

Here are some things to keep in mind from the lender's perspective:

* Usually, a minimum 20% cash down is required (depending on loan type)
* Debt Service Ratio 1.25 (Adjusted Gross Income/Total Debts)
* Industry Experience
* Types of Collateral
* Net Worth

Why is it important? It shows that you can manage and operate your business.

Types of collateral – property (home or commercial building), stocks, equipment, inventory, invoices, blanket lien, cash, bonds, or other investment collateral.

Lenders recommend at least 3-5 years' experience in any industry you are interested in pursuing.

* 0-3 years start up (very risky)
* 3-7 years (moderate risk)
* 7 and above years (low risk)

What is net worth? Total asset - total liability

The Benefits of the lender gatheringaccurate financial information:

* Gives the lender a true general picture of the status of your company and helps calculate a good cash flow.
* Helps to make quality loan decisions, provides reliable information for

annual review, and keeps you out of trouble.

- Helps manage the business properly.
- Helps to get credit line increases for expenses.
- Shows good character (not trying to cheat the government).

Underwriting Criteria

1. Character (honest, capable borrower), a major factor in evaluating the 2wcreditworthiness and trustworthiness of the borrower, is revealed by previous credit history. Even if a loan is collateralized, and is supported by a good cash flow, if the borrower's character is questionable, the loan will not be approved.

2. The purpose of the loan should be explicitly stated, demonstrating both practicality and compliance with legal requirements. Listed below are the most common types of loan request.

    a. Purchase – the purpose is to purchase a commercial property, equipment, vehicle, line of credit, etc.

    b. Refinance Existing Debt – the purpose is to refinance existing debt without any cash-out.

    c. Cash Out Refinance - this loan purpose is the most undesirable transaction out of the 3 transactions. The lender operates with caution when handling a cash-out refinance transaction. The lender wants to ensure that the purpose of the cash-out refinances makes financial sense.

3. Cashflow (cashflow to service the loan) - analyzing cash flow is the heart and soul of the underwriting process. The loan must be carefully examined. The debt service coverage ratio cannot exceed 1.25x. However, some exceptions can be made.

4. Collateral - lenders ensure the collateral's appraised value is reliable when underwriting loans. The lender does an appraisal review of all

real estate and other types of collateral to secure the appraised value is accurate.

5. Capital (borrower's equity) - the borrower must put money down into the project or use the available equity in the property. The borrower's capacity or equity acts as a buffer for the lender if the value of the collateral declines.

Types of Equity

- Cash = cash on hand
- Long-term equity = equity built over time such as real estate
- Short-term equity = equity built over a short-term period such as automobile, equipment, etc.

Loan to Value Ratios

LTV is an important measure of equity in the property.

Calculating the LTV is   a very simple process. It is straightforward. Please see the example below:

Appraised Property Value = $100,000

Lien on property (balance owed) = 0

Available equity in property = $100,000

Lender's LTV Guidelines for Real Estate Property Example

Raw unimproved land	50%	$50,000
Improved Land	65%	$65,000
Non-owner occupied which is investment property	75%	$75,000
Commercial Owner Occupied	80%	$80,000
Commercial Owner Occupied (SBA guarantee)	90%	$90,000

For instance, if you desired to borrow from a commercial owner-occupied property, you would likely have to invest 20% of the purchase price.

The LTV limits are meant to serve as general guidelines however, there are some exceptions made to the guidelines.

Non-Real Estate LTV	
1. CD Secured	100%
2. Commercial Vehicles	80%
3. Machinery and Equipment Appraised Values	75%
4. Inventory	50%
5. U. S. Treasury Securities	75%

Commercial underwriters may review are income assets, debt, credit history, and credit card statements. Underwriting processes are verification of the accuracy of borrower's financial information, credit site inspections, and various other information at the discretion of the underwriter:

1. Verifications = The lender will verify the information the borrower presented as accurate and correct.
2. Credit Reports = The lender will obtain a credit report. The borrower must have a solid credit history.
3. Site Inspection = The lender will perform a site inspection.
4. The lender will perform employment verification as needed.

CHAPTER 5

POST LOAN REQUIREMENTS

Many business owners don't realize that even though the loan has been funded, the lending process is not complete. The lender has some post-loan requirements for which the borrower will be responsible for the life of the loan.

In this section, the post-loan requirements will be explained in detail.

Commercial Loan Annual Reviews

The annual commercial review aims to check the borrower's pulse and the business's healthiness.

Purpose and Benefits of Loan Reviews from the Lender's Perspective

- Monitor asset quality - regular reviews help the lender to accurately access the quality of its loan portfolio.
- Identify problem loans as soon as possible - identifying a problem or negotiating trends sooner rather than later increases the likelihood that steps can be taken to prevent losses.
- Learning opportunity - preparing and reading loan reviews give

lenders the insight to look for other loan opportunities.

- Conduct research - lenders like to research the status of the borrower by obtaining updated information such as the following:

a. Financial Information from the Borrower - business and personal tax returns, including all entities, and a personal financial statement from all borrowers and guarantors.

b. Financial Information on Real Estate Projects - it is important that borrowers submit an accurate summary of income and expenses for real estate collateral if the information is not included in the tax returns. Also, copies of rent rolls and new leases.

c. Insurance - the lender will determine if insurance coverage is enough to protect against loss.

d. Document Review - the lender will review the file to ensure the mortgage is recorded and the title policy is in order, accurate, and has a legal description.

e. Credit Reports - the lender will review personal credit on all borrowers/guarantors to ensure that the financial condition has not deteriorated significantly since the loan originated.

f. Site Inspections - the lender will visit the property to ensure that the property is being maintained. It ensures that the collateral is in good condition.

g. Discussion with Borrowers - Lenders stay in touch to help manage business growth opportunities, build relationships, and solve problems. This contact aids in keeping their hands on the pulse of the business.

Every year, most lenders take each business loan in their portfolios (with a loan balance over $50,000) through an annual review process. The lender looks at the following areas of the business:

1. The lender looks at the cash flow to see if the business can maintain enough to service business and personal debt.
2. The lender looks at the collateral value of the building or equipment securing the loan to ensure the property is maintained and in good condition.
3. The lender looks at the specific industry to ensure that nothing hinders the business owner's ability to repay the loan. For example, Uber and Lift wiped out the Taxicab industry.
4. The lender looks at the risk ratings of the business to see whether it has an acceptable quality.
5. The lender performs a background review of the business to ensure no tax liens, judgments, or court filings have been filed against the company or the owners within that year.
6. The lender sits down with the business owner to review numbers to see if they are trending up or down and to give professional input from a lender's perspective.

To Break the Lending Code, you must have the following:

- The mind of a lender
- The eye of a lender
- The hand of a lender

FAQS/DEFINITIONS

- What should my credit score be? 640 for secured loans and 680 for unsecured loans or lines of credit.
- Do I need collateral? It depends on the type of loan.
- Can I use my business name instead of my personal name? Personal credit will always be reviewed because you are the business.
- How much capital do I need? Generally, 20% down for a loan.
- How long do I need to be in business? Over 2 years.
- Do I need to provide business tax returns? Yes, both personal and business tax returns for 3 years.
- Do I need a business plan to secure a loan? That depends on how long you have been in business or the type of loan.
- Does my spouse have to be a guarantor on the loan? Only if that person owns 20% or more of the business or their income is needed as cash flow.
- What is liquidity? The amount of cash that is easily accessible.

Sources of Funding

- Personal Savings - The first place to look for funding is your savings or equity. Personal resources include profit-sharing or early retirement funds, real estate equity loans, or cash value insurance policies.

- Life Insurance Policies - The owner can borrow against the policy's cash value. This does not include term insurance because it has no cash value.

- Home Equity Loans - A home equity loan is backed by the value of the equity in your home.

- Friends and Relatives - Founders of a startup business may look to private financing sources such as parents, friends, or relatives.

- Equity Financing - means exchanging a portion of the ownership of the business for financial investment. Involves selling a company's equity in return for capital. For example, the owner of company ABC may need to raise capital to fund business expansion. The owner decides to give up 10% ownership of the company and sell it to an investor in return for capital.

- Banks or Credit Unions - are the most commonly used funding sources for small and medium-sized businesses.

- Microloans - are available through specific nonprofit, community-based organizations experienced in lending and business management assistance.

- Commercial Loan Brokers - act as a middleman between lenders and businesses seeking a loan. They help find a lender and package the loan for a fee.

- Venture Capitalists - are looking for technology-driven businesses with high growth potential in information technology, communications, and biotechnology sectors.

- Angel Investors - are generally wealthy individuals or retired company executives who invest directly in small firms owned by others. Angel investors tend to finance the early stages of the business with investments of $25,000 to $100,000. In exchange for risking their money, angel investors reserve the right to supervise the company's management practices. They tend to be low profile.
- Government Backed Loans - Loans guaranteed by the Small Business Administration and the U.S. Department of Agriculture. Please see www.sba.gov, www.va.gov or www.usda.gov.

Here are additional essential things to know to prepare for the growth of your small business and securing capital.

Personal Credit vs Business Credit

As a business owner, it is crucial to understand the difference between your personal and your business credit.

Personal credit is what you build by showing trustworthiness when paying your bills on time. Consistency in payments (from credit cards to automobile loans) will increase your credit rating.

However, it's important to remember your personal credit should be separate from your business credit. You can start building business credit when you have a separate business account.

What Is Business Credit?

Business credit is defined as credit extended by one business to another business. When a creditor extends credit to a borrower, the borrower can buy or lease equipment, purchase goods, inventory, or services, and defer payment over time. Business credit helps the borrower keep more cash for other operating expenses.

A business credit bureau is a storehouse of collected trade and credit information on millions of companies. The business credit bureaus gather credit information as potential creditors so the creditors can make sound credit decisions on credit applications.

Major Business Credit Bureau Agencies in the United States

- **Equifax**
- **Experian**
- **Dun & Bradstreet**

Business Loan Paperwork

Document requirements vary from lender to lender. You might have one or two unexpected requests, but if you are prepared with the following documents, you are most likely covered:

- Business Loan Application
- Personal Financial Statement
- All owners, principals, and officers signed and dated within the last 45 days.
- Management Resume
- History of the Business
- Business Debt Schedule
- Monthly Performance Income Statement for 12 months
- Business Financial Statements (Income Statement, Balance Sheets, and last 3 years of Tax Returns)
- Interim Financial Statement (signed and dated within the last 45 days)
- Business Performance Financial Statement, Balance Sheet, and Cash Flow Projections
- Personal Tax Returns (most recent 3 years)
- Aging of Accounts Receivables and Payable (as of the date of the interim financial statements)

- IRS Form 4506C is a request for transcripts of tax returns

10 Common Mistakes Made When Applying for a Commercial Loan

1. Not knowing your credit scores.
2. Not reading the terms carefully before signing.
3. Not locking the rate.
4. Not explaining what the loan is for
- When applying for a loan, indicate how the money will be used. The lender wants to know precisely what you need and how the funds will meet your need.
5. Making major changes
- Do not open major credit cards or apply for personal loans during the application process.
- Do not make significant personal chargers to your business structure.
- Lenders want to see stability.
6. Applying only to big banks and not to local banks or credit unions
7. Not having your financials up to date.
8. Failing to have some equity in the project.
- Most lenders would like to be 20% cash down.
9. Having no collateral.
10. Not having a business plan.

Types of Business Loans

Commercial Real Estate - loans secured by commercial real estate will be underwritten, emphasizing the borrower's creditworthiness and conventional analysis of the property's cash flow and debt service coverage. Examples of desirable commercial real estate include:
- Rental properties and apartment complexes

- Office buildings and facilities with space leased to tenants
- Properties occupied by an owner/user business
- Facilities used for retail, manufacturing, wholesaling/ distribution, etc.
- Religious facilities and properties
- Land or development loans with specific plans for improvement
- Other types of non-specialized commercial real estate

Equipment - loans secured by equipment will equal the useful economic life of the equipment for terms generally not to exceed 60 months on conventional loans and 120 months on SBA-Secured Loans.

Business-Use Vehicles - loans secured by vehicles will equal the vehicle's useful life do not exceed 60 months on conventional loans and 120 months on SBA-secured loans.

Lines of Credit - the credit committee will consider lines of credit under the same general underwriting guidelines as other business loans, emphasizing the business's operating cash flow. Lines may be secured by other collateral such as real estate, savings, or CD-secured.

Accounts Receivable & Inventory - loans secured by the assignment of accounts receivable and/or inventory evidenced by a general business security agreement with regular and adequately prepared financial statements. Loans based on a formula of accounts receivable, and inventory will be monitored regularly basis through receipt of accounts receivable and payable aging reports, concentrations, and inventory levels, with periodic compliance reports (borrowing base certificates) submitted and signed by a representative of the member business.

Other Loan and Collateral Types - the following may be used to supplement the commercial loan program. These will be used sparingly and typically as additional collateral rather than as the sole collateral for the loan.

Stocks - loans secured by publicly owned individual stocks listed on a major stock exchange and secured by a collateral pledge agreement.

Life Insurance - loans secured by life insurance cash surrender value.

Savings - loans secured by a savings account or certificate of deposit.

Residence - only the business owner's primary residence can be used to secure loans for business purposes..

Letters of Credit - may be issued by the lender as a commercial letter of credit to creditworthy borrowers.

GOVERNMENT-BACKED SBA LOANS: SBA loans carry a guarantee from the Small Business Administration (SBA), a federal government agency. Many SBA programs available, such as the SBA Express Program, where the SBA guarantees up to 50% of the loan. The SBA 7a Program, where the loan is insured up to 75% on commercial real estate, equipment loans, and working capital loans, is typically used for working capital or start-up businesses.

USDA LOANS

This program offers loan guarantees to lenders for loans to rural businesses. They typically come with a 75% guarantee.

UNSECURED LOANS AND LINES OF CREDIT

These loans are mainly used for working capital without holding any collateral.

BUSINESS CREDIT CARD

This should be used only for business purposes.

BUSINESS ACQUISITION LOANS

These are used to acquire a company already up and running or open a new franchise.

TYPES OF DESIRED LOANS WITH LESS RISK

- Owner-occupied commercial real estate
- Professional service firms (medical, dental, legal, accounting, engineering, architecture)
- Manufacturers Wholesalers

TYPES OF UNDESIRABLE LOANS (HIGH RISK)

(Lenders usually approach with caution)

Trucking, restaurants, convenience stores, churches, and other non-profits, construction contractors, home builders, real estate developers, hotels, pawnshops, and businesses less than 2 years old.

Now that you have embarked on this insightful journey through the lend er's intricate mind , I hope that you have acquired a new found unde rstanding of the lending landscape. This acquired knowledge will emp ower you to approach your business decisions with the keen insight of a lender, ensuring the best possible outcomes for your small business. Just as a skilled gardener carefully tend s to the soil, so to should you nurture your small business with the discerning hand of a lender.

REFERENCES

Brandon Metcalf. (2020., July 27th) "82% of small businesses fail because of cash flow problem. https://www.placetechnology.com/blog/82-of-small- businesses-fail-because-of-cash-flow-problems-here-are-3-ways-to-fix- that#:~:text=But%20according%20to%20US%20Bank, company%20ran%20out%20of%20cash.

ABOUT THE AUTHOR

Will M. Campbell, Jr., MA Director

The b1 Foundation

Baton Rouge, Louisiana

Will Campbell previously served as the Vice President for Essential Federal Credit and SBA Manager of Capital One Bank's Small Business Lending Division, governing financial matters with the Small Business Administration. Before joining Capital One, Will served as the Director of the Louisiana Small Business Development Center at Southern University. He was responsible for overseeing and managing the center while providing business consulting for citizens in seven parishes. The center strongly focused on creating entrepreneurs in Baton Rouge and the surrounding areas, especially emphasizing contractual services. Will is an adjunct professor at Southern University, teaching Entrepreneurship in the MBA program.

In addition, Will was the regional manager at Liberty Banks throughout the Baton Rouge and Opelousas regions. He has over 30 years of experience in the financial services industry, including Vice President/ Banking Center Manager for Bank One, and Branch Manager for Wells Fargo Financial.

Mr. Will Campbell is well known for his involvement in the lending industry, economic development programs, and community outreach initiatives. His experience in lending has empowered him to help many small businesses define and achieve their goals. His expertise includes loan packaging, strategic business planning, bank management, and entrepreneurship. He is also the Senior Pastor of Serenity Praise and Worship Tabernacle Church and the CEO of Millennium Consulting Network, Inc. Will has been married to Mary (Myra) Campbell for 25 years. They have three children: Will III, David, and Maya.

Will is most proud of his 17 years as a Captain in the United States Army Reserves, where he served as a Traffic Management Officer and Family Support Liaison. Will received a Master of Arts in Management and Leadership from Liberty University. He received a certificate of Entrepreneurship Educators from Babson College and is pursuing a Ph.D. in Management and Leadership.

For speaking engagements, interviews, and bulk purchases contact Will Campbell at:**breakingthelendingcode@gmail.com**